the craft of coloring

30 FLORAL-INSPIRED GEOMETRIC DESIGNS
an adult coloring book

ISBN-13:978-1519220226
ISBN-10:1519220227

Copyright © 2015 by The Craft of Coloring, All Rights Reserved.
No part of this book may be transmitted in any form or by any means whatsoever without written permission from the author.

DISCOVER THE CRAFT OF COLORING

This book contains 30 Floral-Inspired Geometric Designs to help you relax and bring some color into your life. It was created with the intention to bring you just a little more into the moment and give you the opportunity to create something awesome!

TIPS AND SUGGESTIONS

Try using a variety of different coloring tools such as pencils, pens, crayons, markers, pastels, or even mixing mediums.

By contrasting and blending colors you can create interesting and unique designs.

Try experimenting by adding lighter shades to create the illusion of light.

Feel free to photocopy the pages right from the book so that you can experiment with different color schemes for the same design.

WE'D LOVE TO SEE WHAT YOU CREATE!

Facebook: www.facebook.com/thecraftofcoloring
Instagram: @TheCraftofColoring

Also be sure to subscribe to our newsletter by going to **www.thecraftofcoloring.com**. You'll receive news on our latest projects and we'll let you know when we're running sales!

WANT MORE?

Be sure to check out our other adult coloring books such as:
60 Geometric Patterns & Designs
35 Mandala Designs
32 Animal & Nature Designs
30 Paisley & Henna Designs

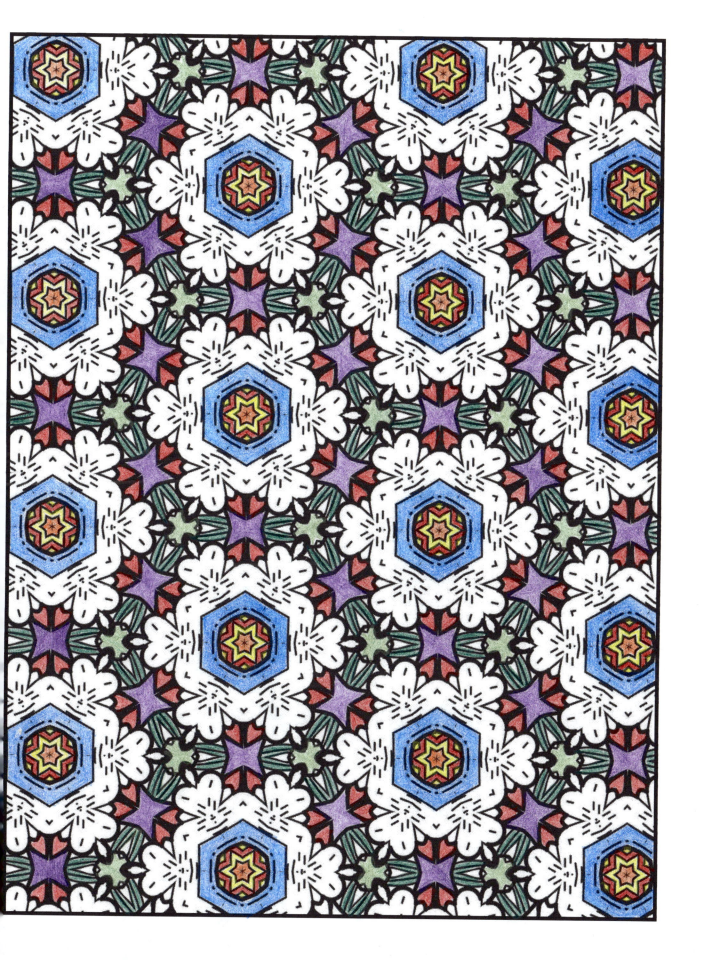

Made in the USA
San Bernardino, CA
29 November 2015